Bible Quiz
from
A to Z

by
V. L. Reece

Bloomington, IN  Milton Keynes, UK

authorHOUSE

AuthorHouse™
1663 Liberty Drive, Suite 200
Bloomington, IN 47403
www.authorhouse.com
Phone: 1-800-839-8640

AuthorHouse™ UK Ltd.
500 Avebury Boulevard
Central Milton Keynes, MK9 2BE
www.authorhouse.co.uk
Phone: 08001974150

First published by AuthorHouse 5/3/2006

ISBN: 1-4259-2036-5 (sc)

Printed in the United States of America
Bloomington, Indiana

This book is printed on acid-free paper.

September, 2005

This is dedicated to my friends and family. It is created in the hope that everyone can enjoy the reading and studying of the Holy Scriptures as much as I did in the making of these quizzes.

To those of you who encouraged and helped me with this endeavor, I say "Thank You!" ...you know who you are.

May God bless you all in good health and peace for all of your days.

In Christian Love,

Virginia

...searched the scriptures daily,
whether those things were so...
John 17:11

ACKNOWLEDGMENTS

Nothing of worth is ever done alone and without the long hours of work done by my son, Terry Trent, I would not have been able to finish this book. Also, thanks go to my daughter-in-law, Marilyn for her cover design ideas. And to all my family and church friends who have been right with me all the way through this work.

I am especially grateful to the Elders of my faith who went out of their way to share their wisdom, help, and encouragement in this endeavor. With my undying gratitude, I pray that God will continue to bless you all.

BIBLE QUIZ

from

A to Z

V. L. Reece, Author

References:
1. King James Translation
2. Strong's Concordance
3. Pictoral Bible Dictionary

First printing September, 2005.

Published by
THE AMERICAN REGISTER
Little Rock, Arkansas
www.americanregister.biz

Send your comments and inquiries to
vreece_quizzes @ sbcglobal.net

BIBLE QUIZ #1

All answers begin with the letter

1. Who was Moses' brother?
2. Who was the first man on earth?
3. Who did Cain kill?
4. Who was married to Sarah?
5. Who was the son of Gideon by a concubine?
6. Which of David's sons was known for his beauty?
7. What is another name for a bottomless pit?
8. What is the area called which was purchased with the money Judas received for betraying Christ?
9. Which son of David did Solomon have killed?
10. In the Old Testament, what sin is punishable by death?
11. Who lied to Peter and the church by pretending to give all he received from the sale of his property and fell down dead?
12. What is a Greek market place called?
13. What was the last name of King Herrod 11?
14. What is the place of animal sacrifice called?
15. What is the word following prayer?
16. Who was the father of the prophet Isaiah?
17. Which apostle was the brother of Simon Peter?
18. What are supernatural beings called?
19. Where were Christians first called Christians?
20. Where did the Ark land after the flood?

BIBLE QUIZ #2

All answers begin with the letter $\mathcal{B}$

1. Who was the prisoner set free instead of Jesus?
2. What did John (son of Elizabeth) do in the wilderness?
3. What god did most people worship before Christianity?
4. What famous tower was built on the plains of Shinar?
5. Where was the home of King Nebuchanezzar?
6. What is the ointment for healing wounds called?
7. Who did Deborah choose to lead the Israelites to war against the Cannanites?
8. What was the surname of the Apostle Peter?
9. Who was the wife of Uriah, a soldier in David's army?
10. What is another word for blessedness?
11. Who was the youngest son of Jacob?
12. What is the name of the "pool" thought to have healing powers?
13. What was the City (location) of Jesus' birth?
14. What is the name of the collection of books recognized as the inspired word of God?
15. Who is the pricipal officer of the church?
16. Who married the widow Ruth?
17. What is an abyss?
18. What is a "gopher" wood that is highly combustible?
19. What is the "Staff of Life" called?
20. What did Christ shed for his people?

BIBLE QUIZ #3

All answers begin with the letter

1. What is the name of a prominent Roman family in the 3rd Century B.C. and later became the name given to any earthly ruler?
2. Who was the first born son of Adam and Eve?
3. What was one of the old names for Palestine, also the name of Ham's son?
4. Who was known as the prince of Judah whom Moses sent to spy out the land of Canaan?
5. Where did Christ make his headquarters during his ministry in Galilee?
6. What is another name for the natural man (as opposed to the spiritual man)?
7. What did Jesus and his earthly father do for a living?
8. What was the Greek name given to the Apostle Peter meaning rock or stone?
9. What was a two-wheeled vehicle drawn by two horses?
10. What is a word meaning "love"?
11. Who was the second son of David and the first born of Abigail?
12. Who was the well known woman whose people informed Paul of contentions in the Corinthian church?
13. Who was God manifested in the flesh?
14. What was Bethlehem also known as?
15. What is God's list of moral laws?
16. Who was the first Gentile convert?
17. What was the beginning of the universe and all matter?
18. Who was the oldest son of Ham?
19. What did God impose upon the serpent in the Garden of Eden?
20. How did Christ die?

BIBLE QUIZ #4

All answers begin with the letter

1. Whose temple did Sampson destroy in Gaza?
2. Which one of Haman's sons was hanged after Esther became queen?
3. Where was Paul (Saul of Tarsus) going when he was struck down by God?
4. Who was the fifth son of Jacob?
5. Who was gifted to interpret dreams and was thrown into a den of lions?
6. Who was Jesse's youngest son, born 1040 B.C.?
7. What did Paul call Phebe?
8. Who was the fouth and greatest of Israel's judges, and also a prophetess?
9. What were the basic laws of the Hebrew state called which was given by GOD to Moses at Mt. Sinai?
10. Who learned the secret of Sampson's strength and brought him to his ruin?
11. Who raised a mob against Paul for his preaching which resulted in damage to his business of making silver images of the goddess Diana?
12. What is another name for evil spirit?
13. What was the plain of the Jordan Sea and the Dead Sea?
14. Who is the evil author of lies?
15. What are the teachers of Christianity called?
16. Who was the Christian disciple, well known for her works of charity, who died and was raised from the dead after Peter prayed for her?
17. How did God communicate with Nebuchadnezzar?
18. What rises to the top as worthless during the melting of metals?
19. What is a beast of burden which has to kneel down to get through a small gate?
20. What was the surname of Thomas?

BIBLE QUIZ #5

All answers begin with the letter

1. What were the people who were the descendants of Esau called?
2. What was the land called where Moses was born?
3. What word is interchangeable with "bishop"?
4. What is the Sovereign decree of GOD to choose out a people for himself called?
5. How many apostles were there after Jesus died?
6. Who was the prophet who foretold of the fate of Jezebel?
7. Who was Hannah's husband?
8. Where did Adam and Eve live before they ate of the forbidden fruit?
9. Who was translated that he should not see death?
10. Who was the son of Seth who lived to be 905 years of age?
11. What are the 21 writings of the New Testament called?
12. Who was the first born twin son of Isaac and Rebecca?
13. Who was the Jewish orphan who became the Queen of Persia?
14. Who did Phillip help to understand what he was reading in the book of Isaiah?
15. Who was Adam's help meet?
16. What is the term designating that which is not in harmony with God's divine order?
17. What is the event which means the "departure" of the Israelites from Egypt?
18. What is another term meaning exclusion from church fellowship?
19. What is one who announces the good news of Jesus Christ called?
20. What is your state of being when you have been driven from your homeland?

BIBLE QUIZ #6

All answers begin with the letter F

1. What is another word for trust and reliance?
2. What happened in the Garden of Eden when Eve ate of the forbidden fruit?
3. What is the cutting-off of food supply in the land known as?
4. What was the abstinence of food and drink for a period of time known as?
5. Fill in the blank, "the ____ of the Lord is the beginning of wisdom".
6. What is another word for partnership or union with other believers?
7. What tree did Jesus cause to wither away immediately after He found it without fruit?
8. What came from the Lord out of Heaven and destroyed the cities of the plain?
9. What offering went to the support of the priesthood in the Old Testament?
10. What term denotes the collection of God's people together?
11. What term is used to describe the deluge which caused water to cover the earth?
12. What did the Lord call the Scribes and the Pharisees?
13. What is a shallow place in a stream where man can cross on foot?
14. John the Baptist was the _____ of Jesus Christ.
15. What is another term for the remission of sins?
16. What do we call unlawful sexual intercourse of an unwed person?
17. What do we call a white resinous substance obtained from a family of balsam trees which is used in perfumes?
18. What was a person called who whitened and cleaned cloth?
19. What was another name for an oven?
20. What is another name for stranger or not native born?

BIBLE QUIZ #7

All answers begin with the letter

1. How did Mary receive the unique message of Jesus' birth?
2. What body of water did Jesus walk upon?
3. What bitter root or herb was offered to Jesus on the cross?
4. What was the pole for executing and exhibiting a victim by impalement?
5. Who assisted Moses in numbering the people?
6. What is a cultivated or hidden piece of ground?
7. What did the children of Israel crave after eating manna for awhile?
8. What city did GOD threaten with destruction by fire through Amos?
9. What is a study of ancestors or descendents called?
10. What term was used for people of non-Israeli descent?
11. Who was the first born son of Moses and Zipporah?
12. What was the name of the place of Jesus' agony and arrest?
13. What made the spies who went into Canaan "feel like grasshoppers"?
14. Who led the famous army of 300 men to war against the Midanites?
15. Where was Jesus Crucified?
16. Who was the giant that David slew?
17. What kind of wood did Noah use to build the Ark?
18. What do we call the story of God's gift of salvation through the person and work of Christ?
19. Salvation is assured by the Sovereign _____ of God.
20. Where is the home of the Helenes?

BIBLE QUIZ #8

All answers begin with the letter ℋ

1. Which prophet asked GOD why the wicked people of Judah went unpunished?
2. What is Esther's Jewish name?
3. What is another name for the place of eternal punishment?
4. Who was Ishmael's mother?
5. What does "praise ye Jehovah" mean?
6. Who was the youngest son of Noah?
7. Who plotted to destroy the Jewish race and was hanged on the same gallows he had built for another man's execution?
8. Who was married to Elkanah and the mother of Samuel?
9. What is the seat of affection called?
10. What term was used for people of non-Israeli descent?
11. Paul was caught up into the third _____ ?
12. What did Paul describe himself as?
13. What was another name for wall or fence or protection?
14. What do you call a doctrine or sect representing a departure from sound doctine?
15. Who schemed and secured the death of John the Baptist?
16. What word means separateness, purity and righteousness?
17. Canaan was said to be "a land flowing with milk and ____".
18. What was the name of the mountain where Moses received his commission?
19. What is a word meaning freedom from pride, lowliness, meekness and mildness?.
20. What does play-acting mean?

BIBLE QUIZ #9

All answers begin with the letter

1. Who was Eli's son who was slain when the ark was taken?
2. What is meant by the departure from true religion, worship of false gods?
3. What word means "GOD is with us"?
4. Which word means to recon, to esteem or to think?
5. Holy Scripture was written by divine _____ .
6. Who was the promised son of Abraham and Sarah?
7. Which prophet spoke as if he was an eyewitness of future events?
8. Who was the son of Hagar and Abraham?
9. John was banished to the _____ of Patmos.
10. Jacob's name was changed by GOD to what?
11. What country is Rome in?
12. What was Judas' last name?
13. Being a child of promise, one is an heir and he has an _____ .
14. In the scriptures man is created by GOD and GOD made him in his own _____ .
15. Since we know not what we should pray for as we ought, the SPIRIT makes _____ for us.?

BIBLE QUIZ #10

All answers begin with the letter

1. Who was Esau's twin brother?
2. Which son of Noah fathered the "isles of the Gentiles"?
3. What was the original name of Jerusalem which means "threshing floor"?
4. What is the Hebrew word for GOD?
5. What is the Greek form of Joshua?
6. Who was the father-in-law of Moses?
7. What are the people of Judea called?
8. Who was the idolatrous wife of Ahab?
9. What was the royal residence of Ahab called?
10. Who was the general-in-chief of David's army?
11. Who was the patriot of Uz who suffered with boils and lost his entire family and fortune in one day?
12. What was the name of Moses' mother?
13. Who baptized Jesus?
14. Who was commissioned to denounce Ninevah and his refusal resulted in his being swallowed by a whale?
15. What body of water did Jesus get baptized in?
16. Who invented the harp and the organ?
17. What was the year called when the land rested and the slaves were freed?
18. Who betrayed Christ for thirty pieces of silver?
19. Deborah was the first female _____ of Israel.
20. What is pardon and acceptance of the just through faith?

BIBLE QUIZ #11

All answers begin with the letter

1. Older Christian women are admonished to teach the younger women to be sober, love their husbands, to love their children and be _____ .
2. Abel was a _____ of sheep.
3. Moses _____ the flock of Jethro his father-in-law and led them to a mountain of God.
4. The vow of a Nazarite was that they (man or woman) could not drink any wine or liquor or eat dried grapes, nor anything from the _____ even the husk.
5. Jesus said to the scribes and Pharisees, "Woe unto you lawyers! For ye have taken away the _____ of _____ : ye entered not in yourselves, and them that were entering in ye hindered."
6. Jesus said to Saul on the road to Damascus, "I am Jesus whom you persecutest: it is hard for thee to _____ against the pricks."
7. While Peter was upon the housetop to pray, he fell into a trance and saw heaven open up and a sheet was let down with all manner of animals on it and a voice came to him and said, Rise, Peter; _____ and eat.
8. "A prophet is not without honor, but in his own country, and among his own _____ , and in his own house."
9. When Paul escaped from a shipwreck and came to an island called Melita, he said the people showed _____ and a fire.
10. God made a covenant with Abraham that in his seed would all the _____ of the earth be blessed.
11. The Apostle Paul admonished his people to Honor all men. Love the brotherhood. Fear God. Honor the _____ .
12. Paul lived two years in Rome in his own hired house and received all who came unto him, preaching the_____ of God.
13. Who was the father of King Saul?
14. Judas betrayed Jesus with a _____ .
15. Paul said as it is written "as I live, saith the Lord, every _____ and every tongue shall confess to God."
16. Paul told Timothy that in the last days man would be ever learning and never be able to come to the _____ of the truth.

BIBLE QUIZ #12

All answers begin with the letter

$\mathcal{L}$

1. Who was Jacob's uncle who tricked him into marrying his elder daughter?
2. What did Jacob see in his Bethel dream?
3. What did John The Baptist call Jesus?
4. What was the language of the Romans?
5. What is a principal which governs one's actions called?
6. Who was Martha and Mary's brother who died and in four days Christ raised him from the dead?
7. Who was Jacob's first wife?
8. What was the main clothing of Elijah and John The Baptist made of?
9. Solomon used cedars from _____ to build the temple in Jerusalem.?
10. Who was the third son of Jacob and Leah whose descendants received a special status in Israel?
11. What book contains the names of God's elect which will not be blotted out?
12. God's command of the forces of nature results in thunder, rain and _____ .
13. What material was the body of Jesus wrapped in for burial?
14. What is the horizontal beam of wood or stone forming the upper part of a doorway called?
15. Which insect did John The Baptist eat?
16. The disciples' prayer is wrongly called what?
17. The communion service begins with the ____ ____.
18. Against Abraham's advice his nephew _____ chose to live in a wicked city.
19. God is _____ .
20. Who was the seller of purple and Paul's first convert in Europe?

BIBLE QUIZ #13

All answers begin with the letter

1. Where was Mary Magdeline born?
2. What are the highest officials in the government who have the power of administering justice?
3. Who are the ungodly nations which are the four corners of the earth and who oppose the people of God?
4. What is a female slave or bondwoman called?
5. Who is the "messenger of Jehovah" and wrote the last book of the Old Testament?
6. What is another name for riches?
7. Who was the elder son of Joseph whom Jacob claimed for himself?
8. What was the crib called where Jesus was born?
9. What food did God provide daily for the Israelites?
10. What name did Naomi adopt instead of her own?
11. What was John's surname?
12. What was the place for trade or things traded?
13. God created man and woman and united them in?
14. Where was Paul taken in Greece to clarify his mysterious teachings?
15. Who was the virgin maiden who gave birth to Jesus?
16. What is the meaning of the annointed one?
17. Who was the son of Enoch and lived for 1000 years?
18. Who became the cheif minister of the king after Haman was hanged?
19. What was the place called where Abraham was told to offer up Isaac?
20. Who delivered the Ten Commandments to the Israelites?

BIBLE QUIZ #14

All answers begin with the letter

1. What scarred Jesus' hands?
2. Who was the apostle Christ called Bartholomew whom he had seen under the fig tree?
3. What is meant by belonging to nature?
4. Because of his residence, Jesus was called a _____ .
5. What king did Daniel interpret a dream for?
6. Christ said "it is easier for a camel to go through the eye of a _____ than for a rich man to enter into the Kingdom of God.?
7. Who was the "cupbearer" to King Artaxerxes?
8. Thou shalt love thy _____ as thyself?
9. What is the beginning of spiritual life in a believer?
10. A collection of 27 documents which is the second part of the Sacred Scriptures is called _____ .
11. Who spoke up for Christ in the Sanhedrin concerning the injustice of condemning a man without a fair trial?
12. What is the "river of Egypt" called?
13. Who was the son of Lamech who was given instructions to build an ark?
14. A good _____ is better than precious ointment and the day of death better than the day of one's birth.
15. Paul told Timothy that people bring _____ into the world.
16. Blessed is the _____ whose God is the Lord; and the people whom he has chosen for his own inheritance.
17. Who was Ruth's mother-in-law?
18. Jesus told a luke warm church that they were poor, and blind, and _____ .
19. _____ the foundation of God standeth sure, knowing this seal The Lord knoweth them that are his.
20. Let everyone that _____ the name of Christ depart from iniquity.

BIBLE QUIZ #15, #16

All answers begin with the letter 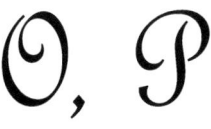 O, P

1. An appeal to God to witness the truth of a statement is called _____ .
2. Who was a gate keeper of Jerusalem in Nehemiah's time?
3. The supreme test of faith in God is _____ .
4. The act of bowing low or prostrating one's self is called _____ .
5. What is the last letter of the Greek alphabet which means the end?
6. God is everywhere at all times, so he is _____ .
7. What is meant by setting aside offices in the church for a certain work by the laying on of hands?
8. Who was the first of 7 "judges" to deliver Israel from foreign oppression?
9. Christ spoke in _____ so that those who had rejected Him were not to know the "mysteries" of the Kingdom.
10. A place of spiritual bliss is called _____ .
11. What is meant by forgiveness and justification?
12. The feast of the unleavened bread is called _____ .
13. The Apostle Paul was exiled to the Isle of _____ .
14. What name was given to Saul of Tarsus?
15. Who was one of Elkanah's wives who bore children & taunted Hannah?
16. What word meaning "the fiftieth day" denoted the Feast of the Harvest?
17. What was the Apostle's name which meant "the rock"?
18. What was the supreme monarch of Egypt called?
19. What mount was Moses on when he was allowed to view the promised land?
20. Who purchased Joseph from the Midanites and made him overseer of his house?
21. What is the field called which the priests bought with Judas' money?
22. What was a person called who makes earthen vessels?
23. The seeking of God's grace, mercy and loving kindness is called _____ .
24. The organized body of church elders is called _____ .
25. What is meant by book of praises?

BIBLE QUIZ #17, #18

All answers begin with the letter Q, R

1. The words of the wise are heard in _____ .
2. What flesh did God tell Moses that He was sending to the Israelites in the wilderness?
3. After Solomon had answered all her questions, who said "only half had been told to her"?
4. Who was the mother of Joseph?
5. Who was the mother of Boaz and was saved from death when she played a roll in the capture of Jericho?
6. What sign reminds us of the covenant from God to Noah that he would never again destroy the earth with water?
7. The redemptive price paid by Christ on the cross for the salvation of his people is called _____ .
8. Who was the mother of Jacob and Esau?
9. God's people are freely justified by grace through _____ that is in Christ Jesus.
10. What body of water did Moses, directed by God, lead the Israelites over dry shod?
11. What is meant by being born again?
12. What is meant by "change of mind" with regard to sin?
13. The entire Bible is a promise of the birth, ministry, death and _____ of Jesus Christ.
14. John wrote the last book of the Bible called _____ .
15. In the 6th and 7th centuries before Christ, the largest government was the _____ .
16. Who was the Moabitess who was the daughter-in-law of Naomi?
17. In the New Testament, what does petra mean?
18. Who was the eldest son of Jacob?
19. In man's relation to God, he who is amoral, unfit with lack of positive holiness is said to be a _____ .
20. Who was the son of Solomon who was his successor to the throne of Israel?

BIBLE QUIZ #19

All answers begin with the letter

1. Who was the wife of Anias who lied to Peter about selling her possessions and was struck dead?
2. What is the Greek word which Christ uttered on the cross meaning "my God, my God, why hast thou forsaken me"?
3. What is the Lord's Day?
4. All of God's people are called _____ ?
5. What was the city where Melchizedek was king?
6. Who enticed Herod with her dancing to behead John the Baptist?
7. Christ made the ultimate _____ by giving his life for the of his people.
8. What man of great strength became enamoured by a woman named delilah?
9. Who wrote the Book of Judges around 1000 B.C.?
10. What was the highest Jewish Tribunal duringh the Greek and Roman periods called?
11. Who was the wife of Abraham?
12. Who was and is the grand adversary of God and Man?
13. Who was the first king of Israel?
14. A Jewish lawyer is a _____ .
15. All of God's children are called _____ .
16. What is another meaning of Messiah?
17. The Holy Bible is also known as the Holy _____ .
18. The first of 6 extended discourses given by Christ is known as what?
19. What animal represents the children of God?
20. Satan is the author of lies and _____ .
21. Who along with his brother Levi massacred the Hivites living in Shechem because of the injury done to their sister Dinah?
22. What was the mount called where God gave Moses the law?
23. Bearing false witness with malicious intent is called what?
24. Who was the wise man who was the second son of David and Bathsheba?
25. The supreme authority of God is also known as what?

BIBLE QUIZ #20

All answers begin with the letter

1. The Jewish worship place in the wilderness was a tent called _____ .
2. Who was the Christian woman who lived in Joppa, made clothing for poor widows and Peter raised from the dead?
3. What was another word for slander?
4. Who was the daughter of Absalom whom her half brother violated?
5. Where was the Apostle Paul born?
6. What is the meaning of self control?
7. Solomon built a great "house" which took seven years: what is it called?
8. What was Paul's vocation?
9. A binding contract or covenant between persons is a _____ .
10. Where was Paul sent away from for preaching Jesus as the Messiah?
11. One of the apostles was known as doubting _____ .
12. Because of their bold or sometimes rash natures, Jesus called James and John the sons of _____ .
13. What river other than the Euphrates watered the garden of Eden?
14. Who was Paul's spiritual child?
15. A writing or giving over by word of mouth to teach generations in the ways of their forefathers is called _____ .
16. "By faith Enoch was _____ that he should not see death".
17. What were Adam and Eve told not to eat the fruit thereof?
18. A definite punishment or chastening from the Lord for misbehavior brings about _____ .
19. The Father, The Son and The Holy Spirit make up the _____ .
20. The exact opposite of lying is _____ .
21. Jesus was arrested and brought before Pilate without a full _____ .
22. Paul said "thanks be unto God who always leadeth us to _____ in Christ.

BIBLE QUIZ #21, #22

All answers begin with the letter $\mathcal{U}$, $\mathcal{V}$

1. The Jewish people referred to the Gentiles as heathen or the _____ .
2. The binding together of God's people is _____ .
3. On Mars Hill Paul found an alter to the _____ .
4. Bread which is not mixed with other ingredients is _____ .
5. The finality of rejecting the testimony of the Holy Spirit regarding the person and work of Jesus Christ is the _____ .
6. The scene of the Lord's Supper is in the _____ .
7. Where was the early home of Abraham?
8. Who was the husband of Bathsheba David had killed?
9. In ancient times the practice of charging interest on money loaned was called _____ .
10. What was the curse word pronounce upon Cain?
11. What is a word which means emptiness, worthlessness and futility?
12. Who was the Persian queen whose place Esther took?
13. Punishment meted out in the sense of retribution is called _____ .
14. The "sorrowful way", the traditional route which our Lord traveled on the day of His crucifixion from the judgement seat of Pilate was _____ .
15. What was Christ offered to drink while upon the cross?
16. What do you call a place for growing grapes?
17. What is another name for snake?
18. Jesus Christ was born of a _____ .
19. A woman of ability and moral worth is a _____ .
20. A voluntary promise to God to perform some service is a _____ .
21. The "non-writing" prophets were the recipients of _____ .

BIBLE QUIZ #23

All answers begin with the letter

1. What is another name for cake?
2. John the Baptist advised the mercenary soldiers to "be content with your _____ .
3. Pharoah sent _____ to help move Jacob and his family.
4. To observe the laws or customs is called what?
5. The blowing of the trumpet announced the call to arms for ____ .
6. After the Lord's Supper, Jesus began to ____ the disciples' feet.
7. John said "In the beginning was the ____ and the ____ was God".
8. Solomon was not only very rich but very _____ .
9. If bread is the staff of life, what is the sustainer of life?
10. When the Egyptians pursued the israelites in their chariots, the Lord took off their _____ .
11. Another name for barren desert or uncultivated region is what?
12. Jesus performed His first miracle at a wedding in Cana by turning _____ into _____ .
13. Another name for grain farming is what?
14. The Magi who came to see the baby Jesus were called what?
15. When we cry ABBA! FATHER! it is the Spirit Himself bearing _____ with our Spirit that we are the children of God.
16. Sarah, Rebecca, Rachel, Deborah, Hannah, Ruth and Esther are outstanding _____ of the Bible.
17. The Israelites were forbidden to wear garments of _____ mixed with linen.
18. Divine honor paid to God is called what?
19. The _____ of God, just pure and holy, is dreadful to evildoers.
20. David said, "I am fearfully and ____ made".
21. The last warning in Revelation is that every man that heareth the _____ of the prophecy of this book and add unto these things, God shall ad unto him the plagues that are written in the Book: or if he takes away any _____ of this prophecy God will take away his part out of the Book of Life, and out of the holy city and from the things which are written in this book.

BIBLE QUIZ #24, #25, #26 *X, Y, Z*

All answers begin with the letter

1. Who was the king who banished Queen Vashti and made Esther queen?
2. Solomon had horses brought out of Egypt and linen _____ .
3. How often did Elkanah and his household go unto the Lord and perform their vows and sacrifice?
4. Jesus is the same _____ , today and forever.
5. James says that no fountain can _____ both salt water and fresh.
6. Christians are not to be unequally _____ together with unbelievers.
7. When Jesus came with the disciples to Gethsemane He said to them, "sit here, while I go to pray _____ .
8. What is another term for thee?
9. Peter preached that Christians should submit _____ to every ordinance of man for the Lord's sake.
10. Paul admonished Timothy to flee from _____ lusts and follow rightousness, faith, charity and peace with them call upon the Lord out of a pure heart.
11. When Jesus passed through Jericho, there was a rich man named _____ in a sycamore tree trying to see Him as he passed by.
12. Who was the father of John the Baptist?
13. What did the apostle Paul say that Israel had but not according to knowlege?
14. Jesus said "as many as I love, I rebuke, and chasten: be _____ therefore, and repent.
15. Who was the father of James and John?
16. What was the surname of Simon, one of Jesus' disciples?
17. What is another name of Jerusalem or City of David?
18. What was the name of Moses' wife?
19. Who was the first born of Canaan?
20. What is the second month of the Hebrew year?
21. What was the priest's name who came to minister to David in Hebron after the death of King Saul?
22. Members of a Jewish patriotic party who resorted to violence and assassinations were called what?

BIBLE QUIZ

A TO Z

Answers

BIBLE QUIZ #1 ANSWERS

1. AARON................................ Exodus 6:20
2. ADAM.................................. Genesis 4:1
3. ABLE.................................... Genesis 4:2
4. ABRAHAM
5. ABIMALECH ....Judges 8:31
6. ABSALOM .... II Samuel 14:25
7. ABYSS
8. ACELDAMA..........................Acts 1:18
9. ADONIJAH ....I Kings 2:19
10. ADULTRY ....Exodus 20:14
11. ANANIAS......................... Acts 4:32-37
12. AGORA
13. AGRIPPA..............................Acts 25:13
14. ALTAR .... Genesis 8:20
15. AMEN .... Matthew 6:13
16. AMOZ II.................................Kings 19:2
17. ANDREW...................... Matthew 10:12
18. ANGELS.......................Psalms 148:2-5
19. ANTIOCH....................... Acts 11:19-26
20. ARARAT .... Genesis 8:4

BIBLE QUIZ #2 ANSWERS

1. BARABAS .... Matthew 12:27
2. BAPTIZED .... Mark 1:4
3. BAAL .... Numbers 22:41
4. BABEL .... Genesis 11:1-9
5. BABYLON .... II Kings
6. BALM OF GILEAD .... Genesis 37:25
7. BARAK .... Judges 4:5
8. BAR-JONA .... Matthew 16:17
9. BATHSHEBA .... II Samuel 1:6
10. BEATITUDE .... Psalms 32
11. BENJAMIN .... Genesis 35:17
12. BETHESDA .... John 5:16
13. BETHLEHEM .... Luke 2
14. BIBLE
15. BISHOP .... I Timothy 3:17
16. BOAZ .... Ruth 3:17
17. BOTTOMLESS PIT .... Deut. 27:17
18. BRIMSTONE .... Rev 20:10
19. BREAD .... Exodus 12
20. BLOOD .... Genesis to Revelations

BIBLE QUIZ #3 ANSWERS

1. CAESAR .... Matthew 12:17-21
2. CAIN .... Hebrews 11:4
3. CANAAN .... Genesis 9:18,22; 10:6
4. CALEB .... Numbers 13:6
5. CAPERNUM .... Matthew 4:13
6. CARNAL .... Corintians 2:14
7. CARPENTRY .... Matthew 13:55
8. CEPHAS .... John 1:42
9. CHARIOT .... Genesis 41:43
10. CHARITY .... I Corinthians 13
11. CHILEAD .... II Samuel 3:3
12. CHLOE .... I Corinthians 1:11
13. CHRIST .... Phillipians 2:6-7
14. CITY OF DAVID .... Luke 2:4
15. COMMANDMENTS ...... Exodus 19:9-25
16. CORNELIUS .... Acts 10:44-47
17. CREATION .... Genesis 1
18. CUSH .... Genesis 10:6-8
19. CURSE .... Genesis 3:14
20. CRUCIFIXION .... Matthew 27:35

BIBLE QUIZ #4 ANSWERS

1. DAGON ....Judges 16:30
2. DALPHON .... Esther 9:6-30
3. DAMASCUS........................ Acts 9:6-13
4. DAN .... Genesis 46
5. DANIEL.................................... Daniel 4
6. DAVID .... II Samuel 5:4
7. DEACONESS....................... Romans 16
8. DEBORAH ....Judges 4,5
9. DECALOGUE .... Exodus 20
10. DELILAH.......................Judges 16:4-20
11. DEMETRIUS .... Acts 19:23-27
12. DEMON ....Acts 16:16
13. DESERT .... Ezekiel 47:8
14. DEVIL...............................Timothy 3:11
15. DISCIPLES...................... Matthew 9:14
16. DORCUS .... Acts 9:36-43
17. DREAMS........................Daniel 2:1-45
18. DROSS .... Isaiah 1:22-25
19. DROMEDARY............. (1-hump camel)
20. DIDYMUS ....John 11:16-20

BIBLE QUIZ #5 ANSWERS

1. EDOMITES ....Genesis 25:30
2. EGYPT.. Genesis
3. ELDER...................................Acts 14:23
4. ELECTION .... John 6:37, Eph. 1:4
5. ELEVEN ....Acts 1:26
6. ELIJAH ....II Kings 9:36
7. ELKANAH .... I Samuel 1:1-2
8. EDEN ....Genesis 2:8-14
9. ENOCH .... Hebrews 11:5-6
10. ENOS .... Genesis 4:26
11. EPISTLES..................*any good dictionary*
12. ESAU................................Genesis 25:24
13. ESTHER .... The Book of Esther
14. ETHIOPIAN EUNICH .... Deut. 23:1
15. EVE ....Genesis 2:20,23
16. EVIL .... Romans 8:18-22
17. EXODUS................................ I Kings 6:1
18. EXCOMMUNICATION.......Luke 6:22
19. EVANGELIST................Ephesians 4:11
20. EXILE ....*any good dictionary*

BIBLE QUIZ #6 ANSWERS

1. FAITH....................................Romans 3:3
2. FALL OF MAN .... Genesis 3
3. FAMINE ....Genesis 12:10
4. FASTING...............................Isaiah 58:3
5. FEAR.................................. Proverbs 9:10
6. FELLOWSHIP...............II Cor. 6:14-18
7. FIG .... Matthew 21:19
8. FIRE ....Genesis 19:24
9. FIRST FRUITS.................Deut. 26:1-11
10. FLOCK................................ Isaiah 40:11
11. FLOOD .... Genesis 7:11
12. FOOLS .... Matthew 23:17
13. FORD .... Joshua 2:7
14. FORERUNNER ....Hebrews 6:21
15. FORGIVENESS ....Luke 17:4
16. FORNICATION........... Ephesians 5:3-4
17. FRANKINCENSE ....Isaiah 60:6
18. FULLER..................................Isaiah 7:3
19. FURNACE.........................Genesis 15:17
20. FOREIGNER ....Genesis 31:15

BIBLE QUIZ #7 ANSWERS

1. GABRIEL .... Luke 1:26-38
2. GALILEE .... Matthew 14:22-34
3. GALL .... Matthew 27:34
4. GALLOWS .... Esther 5:14, 6:14
5. GAMALIEL .... Numbers 1:10
6. GARDEN .... Proverbs 24:31
7. GARLIC .... Numbers 11:5
8. GAZA .... Amos 1:6
9. GENEAOLOGY .... I Chron. 4:33
10. GENTILES .... Romans 1:16
11. GERSHOM .... Exodus 2:22
12. GETHSEMANE ... Matthew 26:36, 36:56
13. GIANTS .... Numbers 13:33
14. GIDEON .... II Samuel 7:9-14
15. GOLGOTHA .... Luke 23:23
16. GOLIATH .... I Samuel 17
17. GOPHER .... Genesis 6:14
18. GOSPEL ...... Matthew, Mark, Luke & John
19. GRACE .... Luke 1:30
20. GREECE .... Acts 16:1

BIBLE QUIZ #8 ANSWERS

1. HABAKKUK................ Habakkuk 1 & 2
2. HADASSAH........................ Esther 2:7
3. HADES .... Revelations 1:18
4. HAGAR .... Genesis 16:7-14
5. HALLELUJAH............... Psalms 150:1,6
6. HAM .... Genesis 10:6-20
7. HAMAN .... Esther 7
8. HANNAH........................... I Samuel 1:2
9. HEART .... Genesis 6:5
10. HEATHEN .... John 7:35
11. HEAVEN .... II Corinthians 2:12
12. HEBREW of HEBREWS Phil.3:4-6
13. HEDGE .... Psalms 80
14. HERESY .... Acts 24:14
15. HERODIAS........................... Luke 3:19
16. HOLY .... Exodus 15:11
17. HONEY .... Exodus 3, Ezekiel 20:15
18. HOREB .... Exodus 3:1
19. HUMILITY .... Isaiah 57:15
20. HYPOCRISY .... II Timothy 3:5

BIBLE QUIZ #9 ANSWERS

1. INCHABOD.....................I Samuel 4:21
2. IDOLATRY ....Judges 6:25-32
3. IMMANUEL ....Isaiah 7:14
4. IMPUTE .... Romans 4:6-25
5. INSPIRATION.............Matthew 19:4-5
6. ISAAC ....Genesis 17:17
7. ISAIAH ....Isaiah
8. ISHMAEL .... Genesis 16:1
9. ISLE...............................Revelations 1:9
10. ISRAEL ....Genesis 32:28
11. ITALY..Acts 18:2
12. ISCARIOT .... Matthew 4
13. INHERITANCE.................... Mark 12:7
14. IMAGE .... Genesis 1:26
15. INTERCESSION ....Romans 8:26

BIBLE QUIZ #10 ANSWERS

1. JACOB .... Genesis 24:24
2. JAPETH .... Genesis 10:1-5
3. JEBUS .... Joshua 15:8
4. JEHOVAH .... Exodus 6:3
5. JESUS .... Numbers 13:16
6. JETHRO .... Enoch 2:8
7. JEWS .... II Kings 16:6
8. JEZEBEL .... I Kings 16:29-33
9. JEZREEL .... Joshua 19:18
10. JOAB .... II Samuel 2:18-32
11. JOB .... Genesis 36:33
12. JOCHEBED .... Exodus 6:20
13. JOHN THE BAPTIST .... Matthew 3
14. JONAH .... Jonah
15. JORDAN RIVER .... Matthew 3:13
16. JUBAL .... Genesis 4:19-21
17. JUBILEE .... Leviticus 26:8-25
18. JUDAS .... Matthew 10:4
19. JUDGE .... Judges 4,5
20. JUSTIFICATION .... Romans 3:20-31

BIBLE QUIZ #11 ANSWERS

1. KEEPERS AT HOME .... Titus 2:3-5
2. KEEPER .... Genesis 4:2
3. KEPT .... Exodus 3:1
4. KERNELS .... Numbers 6:1-4
5. KEY...KNOWLEDGE .... Luke 11:52
6. KICK .... Acts 9:5
7. KILL .... Acts 10:9-13
8. KIN .... Mark 6:4
9. KINDNESS...KINDLED .... Acts 28:1-2
10. KINDREDS .... Acts 3:25
11. KING .... I Peter 2:17
12. KINGDOM .... Acts 28:30-31
13. KISH .... I Samuel 9:1
14. KISS .... Luke 22:47
15. KNEE SHALL BOW TO ME ...... Romans 14:11
16. KNOWLEDGE .... II Timothy 3:7

BIBLE QUIZ #12 ANSWERS

1. LABAN .... Genesis 27
2. LADDER ....Genesis 28:12
3. LAMB OF GOD ....John 1:29,36
4. LATIN...................................Luke 23:38
5. LAW .... Romans 7:23
6. LAZARUS ....John 11:1-12
7. LEAH ....Genesis 29:34
8. LEATHER .... Matthew 3:4, II Kings 1:8
9. LEBANON.........................II Kings 14:9
10. LEVI ....Genesis 29:34
11. LIFE .... Rev. 3:5, 13:8, 17:8, 2:15
12. LIGHTNING ....Job 28:16
13. LINEN............................ Matthew 27:59
14. LINTEL .... Exodus 12:22,23
15. LOCUSTS................................ Mark 1:6
16. LORD'S PRAYER ....Matthew 6:9-13
17. LORD'S SUPPER.......... I Cor. 11:27-29
18. LOT .... Genesis 13:5-13
19. LOVE ....John 17:24
20. LYDIA..............................Acts 16:13,15

BIBLE QUIZ #13 ANSWERS

1. MAGDALA .... Acts 16:20,22,35
2. MAGISTRATES .... Acts 16:20,22,35
3. MAGOG .... Revelations 20:8
4. MAIDEN .... Exodus 2:5
5. MALACH .... Malachi
6. MAMMON .... Matthew 6:24
7. MANASSAH ..... Gen.41:51, & 48:17-22
8. MANGER .... Luke 2:7
9. MANNA .... Numbers 11:9
10. MARA .... Ruth 1:20
11. MARK .... Acts 12:12,25
12. MARKET .... Ezekiel 27:13,17,19
13. MARRIAGE .... Genesis 12:26
14. MARS HILL .... Acts 17:16-34
15. MARY .... Matthew 1,2 & Luke 1,2
16. MESSIAH .... John 1:41
17. METHUSELAH .... Genesis 5:22-27
18. MORDECAI .... Esther 8
19. MORIAH .... Genesis 22:2
20. MOSES .... Exodus 20-24

BIBLE QUIZ #14 ANSWERS

1. NAILS ....John 20:25
2. NATHANIEL.........................John 1:50
3. NATURAL................... Romans 1:26-27
4. NAZARENE...........................Acts 2:22
5. NEBUCHADNEZZAR.......... Daniel 2
6. NEEDLE........................ Matthew 19:24
7. NEHEMIAH ....Nehemiah 1:11, 2:1
8. NEIGHBOR ...... Lev. 19:18, Matt. 19:19
9. NEW BIRTH........................John 3:3,5,6
10. NEW TESTAMENT..... New Testament
11. NICODEMUS ....John 7:25-44
12. NILE..................................Genesis 15:18
13. NOAH .... Genesis 6:14-16
14. NAME........................... Ecclesiastes 7:1
15. NOTHING ....I Timothy 6:7
16. NATION .... Psalms 33:12
17. NAOMI ....Ruth
18. NAKED........................Revelations 3:17
19. NEVERTHELESS .... II Timothy 2:19
20. NAMETH.................... II Timothy 2:19

BIBLE QUIZ #15-#16 ANSWERS

1. OATH.................................Genesis 21:23
2. OBADIAH .... Nehemiah 12:25
3. OBEDIENCE ....I Samuel 28:18
4. OBIESENCE .... Genesis 42:6
5. OMEGA.......................Revelations 1:8
6. OMNIPRESENCE .... Psalms 132:7, 9:7
7. ORDINATION...............I Timothy 4:14
8. OTHNIEL .... I Chronicles 4:15
9. PARABLES .... Matthew 13:11
10. PARADISE ....Luke 23:43
11. PARDON ....Romans 3:25
12. PASSOVER...................Leviticus 25:5-8
13. PATMOS....................Revelations 1:9
14. PAUL ....Acts
15. PENINNAH .... I Samuel 1:2-7
16. PENTECOST................... Exodus 23:16
17. PETER ....Acts 15:14
18. PHAROAH.................Genesis 12:10-20
19. PISGAH.................... Deuteronomy 3:27
20. PONTIPHER ....Genesis 39:1-20
21. POTTER'S FIELD.......... Matthew 27:7
22. POTTER......................Romans 9:20-23
23. PRAYER........................... Psalms 63:1-8
24. PRESBYTERY ....I Timothy 4:14
25. PSALMS .... Psalms

BIBLE QUIZ #17-#18 ANSWERS

1. QUIET .... Ecclesiastes 9
2. QUAIL .... Exodus 16:13
3. QUEEN OF SHEBA.......... I Kings 10:7
4. RACHEL ....Genesis 29:6,16,18
5. RAHAB .... Joshua 2:1
6. RAINBOW .... Genesis 9:8-17
7. RANSOM .... Mark 10:45
8. REBECCA .... Genesis 22:20-24
9. REDEMPTION ...... I Cor. 6:20, John 3:17
10. RED SEA ....Exodus 13:17-18
11. REGENERATION........ Matthew 19:28
12. REPENTANCE ....Acts 2:38
13. RESURECTION .... King James Bible
14. REVELATIONs....................Revelations
15. ROMAN EMPIRE....Old & New Testament
16. RUTH ....Ruth
17. ROCK........................... Matthew 7:24,25
18. REUBEN............................Genesis 29:32
19. REPROBATE .... Romans 1:28
20. REHOBOAM .... I Kings 14:21

BIBLE QUIZ #19 ANSWERS

1. SAPPHIRA .... Acts 5:1-11
2. SABACHTHANI .... Matthew 27:46
3. SABBATH.................................Acts 2:1
4. SAINTS .... I Corinthians 1:2
5. SALEM ....Genesis 14:18
6. SALOME ....Matthew 14:3-11
7. SACRIFICE ....Luke 19:10
8. SAMSON ....Judges 16:1-31
9. SAMUEL .... Samuel
10. SANHEDRIN ....Matthew 16:21
11. SARAH..........................Genesis 11:29
12. SATAN........................... I Kings 11:14
13. SAUL ....I Samuel 9
14. SCRIBE .... Matthew 22:35
15. SAINTS .... Romans 1:7
16. SAVIOUR............................ Titus 1:4
17. SCRIPTURES.................II Peter 1:20
18. SERMON ON THE MOUNT . Matthew 5,6,7
19. SHEEP..........................John 21:15-17
20. SIN ....Holy Bible
21 SIMEON .... Genesis 34:24-31
22. SINAI............................. Exodus 19:3
23. SLANDER ....Leviticus 19:16
24. SOLOMON .... I Samuel 12:24-25
25. SOVERIGNTY OF GOD... II Cor. 6:18

BIBLE QUIZ #20 ANSWERS

1. TABERNACLE .... Exodus 25:40
2. TABITHA .... Acts 9:36-43
3. TALEBEARING Prov.11:13, Tim5:13
4. TAMAR......................II Samuel 13:1-33
5. TARSUS .... Acts 21:39
6. TEMPERANCE.................... Acts 24:25
7. TEMPLE........................... I Kings 6:38
8. TENT MAKER .... Acts 18:3
9. TESTAMENT ....I Corinthians 11:25
10. THESALONICA .... Acts 17:5-9
11. THOMAS .... John 20:25-29
12. THUNDER........Luke 9:54, Matt.20:20-23
13. TIGRIS............................... Genesis 2:14
14. TIMOTHY ....I Timothy 1:2
15. TRADITIONS................. Galations 1:14
16. TRANSLATED .... Hebrews 11:5
17. TREE OF KNOWLEDGE.... Gen.2:9,22,25
18. TRIBULATION .... Romans 2:9
19. TRINITY .... Matthew 28:18-20
20. TRUTH............................ Hebrews 6:18
21. TRIAL .... John 18:29-32
22. TRIUMPH............... II Corinthians 2:14

BIBLE QUIZ #21-#22 ANSWERS

1. UNCIRCUMCIZED.... Jud,14:3, Rom.4:9
2. UNITY .... Ephesians 4:13
3. UNKNOWN GOD .... Acts 17:23
4. UNLEAVENED BREAD...... I Cor.5:7,8
5. UNPARDONABLE SIN...... Luke 12:10
6. UPPER ROOM .... Luke 22:12
7. UR OF THE CHALDEES ... Gen.11:28-31
8. URIAH .... II Samuel 11:11
9. USURY .... Nehemiah 5:10,12
10. VAGABOND .... Genesis 4:12
11. VANITY .... Book of Ecclesiastes
12. VASHTI.............................. Esther 1:11
13. VENGEANCE .... Judges 5:17
14. VIA DOLOROSA .... Matthew 27:26,31
15. VINEGAR .... Matthew 27:34
16. VINEYARD .... Genesius 14:18
17. VIPER .... *Any Good Dictionary*
18. VIRGIN........................... Matthew 1:23
19. VIRTUOUS WOMAN .... Ruth 3:11
20. VOW............................... Genesis 28:20
21. VISIONS .... Isaiah 1:1

BIBLE QUIZ #23 ANSWERS

1. WAFERS .... I Chronicles 23:29
2. WAGES .... Luke 3:14
3. WAGONS .... Genesis 45:19-46
4. WALK.................................... Acts 21:21
5. WAR .... Judges 3:27
6. WASH .... John 13:5
7. WORD_WORD .... John 1:1
8. WISE.................................. I Kings 3:12
9. WATER .... Ezekiel 16:4-9
10. WHEELS .... Exodus 14:24,25
11. WILDERNESS.................... Deut. 32:10
12. WATER_WINE................... John 2:2-11
13. WINNOWING ...... Any Good Dictionary
14. WISE MEN .... Matthew 2:1-16
15. WITNESS .... Romans 8:15,16
16. WOMEN........................... Exodus 2:1-9
17. WOOL .... Deuteronomy 22:11
18. WORSHIP .... John 20:19
19. WRATH .... Numbers 11:1-10
20. WONDERFULLY.......... Psalms 139:14
21. WORDS_WORDS .... Rev. 22:18-19

BIBLE QUIZ #24 #25 #26 ANSWERS

1. XERSES_AHASURUS .... Esther 1:19
2. YARN................................. I Kings 12:28
3. YEARLY............................I Samuel 1:21
4. YESTERDAY.....................Hebrews 13:8
5. YIELD ....James 3:12
6. YOKED ....II Corinthians 6:14
7. YONDER....................... Matthew 26:36
8. YOU..........................II Corinthians 12:9
9. YOURSELVES .... I Peter 2:19
10. YOUTHFUL .... II Timothy 2:22
11. ZACCHAEUS .... Luke 19:1-5
12. ZACHARIAS ....Luke 1:5
13. ZEAL ....Romans 10:1-2
14. ZEALOUS .... Rev. 3:19
15. ZEBEDEE .... Matthew 4:21
16. ZELOTES.............................Luke 6:15
17. ZION................................ II Samuel 5:7
18. ZIPPORAH .... Exodus 2:21
19. ZIDON........................ I Chronicles 1:13
20. ZIF.. I Kings 6:1
21. ZADOK .... I Chronicles 12:28
22. ZEALOTS .... Any Good Dictionary

BIBLE QUIZ

Part II

ANGELS

(Choose a, b or c for correct answer)

1. Who is the archangel?
   a. Jude 3:10
   b. Jude 1:9
   c. John 3:11

2. Do angels marry or die?
   a. John 3:1
   b. Rev. 3:10
   c. Luke 20:34-36

3. When were angels created?
   a. Exodus 3:11
   b. Job 38:7
   c. Gen. 38:2

4. How are angels described?
   a. Heb. 1:14
   b. Job 37:1
   c. Peter 1:11

5. Angels possess superhuman intellegence, are they omniscient?
   a. Gen. 35:1
   b. Matt. 24:36
   c. Job 3:11

6. Can we number the angels?
   a. John 3:11
   b. Matt. 24:2
   c. Rev 5:11

7. Are angels created holy?
a. Jude 6
b. Exodus 3:10
c. Daniel 3:10

8. Did some angels fall from their state of innocence?
a. Gen. 3:2
b. Exodus 35:11
c. II Peter 2:4

9. What is the work or purpose for God's good angels?
a. Mark 10:11, Acts 10:1, Romans 10:1
b. Matt. 18:10, Rev. 5:11, Heb. 1:6
c. Acts 11:12, Rev. 6:10

10. Does God use angels to punish his enemies?
a. II Kings 19:35, Acts 12:23
b. John 3:1, Rev. 22:1
c. Romans 1:11, John 3:10

11. Did angels have a large place in the life and ministry of Christ?
a. Mark 1:10, John 3:2, Luke 10:11
b. Matt. 4:11, Luke 22:43, Matt. 28:2-7
c. Acts 3:11, John 3:10, Romans 3:8

12. What is the purpose of evil angels?
a. Genisis 3:11
b. Exodus 3:10
c. Romans 8:38

13. Do evil angels oppose good angels in their work?
a. Daniel 10:12-13
b. Genisis 35:2
c. Isaiah 4:5

14. Do evil angels inflict diseases upon mankind?
a. Matt 3:22
b. Luke 1:1
c. Luke 13:11,16

15. Do angels guide the affairs of nations?
a. John 3:15
b. Dan. 10:12,13,20
c. Proverbs 10:12,14,16

16. Do evil angels tempt man to sin?
a. Matt. 4:3, John 13:27, I Peter 5:8
b. Mk. 3:11, John 3:1, Acts 3:15
c. Romans 3:16, Rev. 4:22, Jude 1

17. Was Gabriel a messenger of God?
a. Matt. 3:24
b. Luke 1:19
c. Matt. 24:3

18. Who interpreted Daniel's dream?
a. Daniel 1:10
b. Daniel 8:16
c. Daniel 1:15

19. Who announced the birth of Jesus to Mary?
a. Luke 1:26-38
b. Luke 3:11
c. Luke 15:1

20. Scripture shows that good angels will continue in the service of God in the future age, where will the evil angels be?
a. Mark 15:1
b. Matt. 25:41
c. Romans 8:12

PHRASES

(Some Old Testament Phrases used today)

1. The fat of the land
a. Gen. 45:18
b. Gen. 35:2
c. Gen. 40:16

2. By the skin of one's teeth.
a. Job 19:20
b. Job 18:2
c. Job 10:1

3. Pride goeth before a fall.
a. Proverbs 6:5
b. Proverbs 1:10
c. Proverbs 6:18

4. Eat, drink and be merry.
a. Eccl. 10:11
b. Eccl. 8:15
c. Exodus 10:11

5. A fly in the ointment.
a. Eccl. 10:1
b. Eccl. 15:1
c. Eccl. 15:6

6. Cast your bread upon the waters.
a. Exodus 10:11
b. Eccl. 10:11
c. Eccl. 11:1

7. A drop in the bucket.
a. Isaiah 40:15
b. Isaiah 40:20
c. Isaiah 20:10

SAYINGS

(Some New Testament Sayings used today)

1. A thorn in the flesh.
a. I Cor. 12:7
b. II Cor. 12:7
c. II Cor. 12:23

2. All things to all men.
a. II Cor. 13:1
b. II Cor. 9:1
c. I Cor. 9:22

3. Salt of the earth.
a. Matt. 1:15
b. Matt. 5:13
c. Matt. 2:11

4. The straight and narrow.
a. Matt. 1:11
b. Matt. 7:11
c. Matt. 7:14

5. A wolf in sheep's clothing.
a. Matt. 7:15
b. Matt. 7:20
c. Matt. 25:1

6.   The blind leading the blind.
a.   Matt. 20:1
b.   Mark 1:11
c.   Matt. 15:14

7.   The Good Samaritan.
a.   Luke 10:30
b.   Luke 20:10
c.   Luke 15:30

8.   The powers that be.
a.   Romans 8:15
b.   Romans 13:1
c.   Romans 15:1

PSALMS

(Choose a, b or c for correct answer)

1. In which chapter do you find references to God's word, statutes, promises, decrees, laws, God's ways or commands?
a. Psalm 119
b. Psalm 8
c. Psalm 29

2. For a day in thy courts is better than a thousand...
a. Psalm 2:20
b. Psalm 80:4
c. Psalm 84:10

3. As the heart panteth after the water brooks, so panteth my soul after Thee, O God.
a. Psalm 40:1
b. Psalm 38:1
c. Psalm 42:1

4. Out of the mouths of babes and sucklings hast thou ordained strength because of thine enemies.
a. Psalm 2:4
b. Psalm 8:2
c. Psalm 28:1

5. The wicked shall be turn into hell, and all the nations that forget God.
a. Psalm 9:17
b. Psalm 18:11
c. Psalm 20:1

6.   The fool hath said in his heart, "There is no God".
a.   Psalm 2:12
b.   Psalm 14:1
c.   Psalm 16:2

7.   Keep me as the apple of the eye; hide me under the shadow of thy wings.
a.   Psalm 8:14
b.   Psalm 17:8
c.   Psalm 19:2

8.   Let the words of my mouth and the meditation of my heart be acceptable in thy sight, O Lord, my strength, and my redeemer.
a.   Psalm 100:1
b.   Psalm 20:1
c.   Psalm 19:14

9.   The Lord is my Shepherd, I shall not want.
a.   Psalm 29:20
b.   Psalm 23:1
c.   Psalm 25:1

10. Remember not the sins of my youth, nor my transgressions: according to thy mercy remember thou me for thy goodness sake, O Lord.
a.   Psalm 25:7
b.   Psalm 28:1
c.   Psalm 40:2

11. Wait on the Lord: be of good courage, and he shall strengthen thine heart: Wait, I say, on the Lord.
a. Psalm 3:20
b. Psalm 27:14
c. Psalm 28:28

12. Into thine hand I commit my spirit: thou hast redeemed me, O Lord God of truth.
a. Psalm 4:20
b. Psalm 18:15
c. Psalm 31:5

13. I will instruct thee and teach thee in the way which thou shalt go: I will guide thee with mine eye.
a. Ps. 28:14
b. Ps. 32:8
c. Ps. 40:4

14. Blessed is the nation whose God is the Lord; and the people whom he hath chosen for his own inheritance.
a. Ps. 33:12
b. Ps. 38:12
c. Ps. 40:12

15. Delight thyself also in the Lord; and he shall give thee the desires of thine heart.
a. Ps. 8:15
b. Ps. 37:4
c. Ps. 14:15

16. I have been young, and now I am old; yet I have not seen the righteous forsaken, nor his seed begging bread.
a.   Ps. 30:1
b.   Ps. 10:12
c.   Ps. 37:25

17. In Thee, O Lord, do I put my trust: Let me never be put to confusion.
a.   Ps. 10:2
b.   Ps. 71:1
c.   Ps. 35:1

18. For he shall give his angels charge over thee, to keep thee in all thy ways.
a.   Ps. 80:1
b.   Ps. 82:4
c.   Ps. 91:11

19. Make a joyful noise unto the Lord, all ye lands.
a.   Ps. 100:1
b.   Ps. 98:2
c.   Ps. 80:1

20. O give thanks unto the Lord, for he is good, for his mercy endureth forever.
a.   Ps. 119:18
b.   Ps. 123:2
c.   Ps. 107:1

21. THIS IS THE DAY WHICH THE LORD HATH MADE; WE WILL REJOICE AND BE GLAD IN IT.
a. Ps. 100:3
b. Ps. 118:24
c. Ps. 10:12

22. "FOR HIS MERCY ENDURETH FOREVER" (AT THE END OF EACH VERSE)
a. Ps. 28:1-28
b. Ps. 135:1-21
c. Ps. 136:1-26

23. Let everything that hath breath praise the Lord, Praise ye the Lord.
a. Ps. 29:1
b. Ps. 150:6
c. Ps. 148:1

24. The Lord preserveth the strangers; he relieveth the fatherless and widow: but the way of the wicked he turneth upside down.
a. Ps. 146:9
b. Ps. 147:9
c. Ps. 150:3

25. I was glad when they said unto me, let us go into the house of the Lord.
a. Ps. 28:3
b. Ps. 122:1
c. Ps. 123:5

WOMEN OF THE BIBLE

Where are these passages found?

(Choose a, b or c for correct answer)

1. Abigail:
a. I Sam. 20:1
b. I Kings 2:1
c. I Sam. 25:3

2. Bath-Sheba:
a. I Sam. 20:1
b. II Sam. 11
c. II Sam. 10

3. Bernice:
a. Acts 2:3
b. Acts 5:10
c. Acts 12:1

4. Chloe:
a. I Cor. 1:11
b. Acts 10:12
c. I Cor. 3:15

5. Claudia:
a. II Tim. 20:1
b. II Tim. 4:21
c. I Tim. 10:11

6. Damaris:
a. Acts 3:10
b. Acts 17:34
c. Acts 4:4

7. Deborah:
a. Judges 4-5
b. Judges 6-8
c. Judges 8

8. Delilah:
a. Judges 15:3
b. Judges 16:4-20
c. Judges 17:14-15

9. Dorcas:
a. Acts 5:10
b. Acts 16:4-6
c. Acts 9:36-43

10. Elizabeth:
a. Luke 1:5-17
b. Luke 5:6
c. Luke 10:11

11. Esther:
a. Sam. 15:16
b. Book of Ruth
c. Book of Esther

12. Eunice:
a. Rom. 10:11
b. Acts 16:1
c. Acts 4:10

13. Euodias:
a. Philemon 2:4
b. Philemon 2:10
c. Philemon 4:2

14. Eve:
a. Gen. 2:25
b. Gen. 2:11
c. Gen. 3:6

15. Hagar:
a. Gen. 5:11
b. Gen.16: 1-16
c. Gen. 16:1

16. Hannah:
a. Ex. 3:30
b. I Sam. 1:11
c. I Sam:1:1

17. Herodias:
a. Luke 3:19-20
b. Luke 10:20-21
c. Luke 15:11

18. Jezebel:
a. 1 Kings 1:11
b. 1 Kings 16:32
c. 1 Kings 15:15

19. Joanna:
a. Luke 3:2
b. Luke 15:16-17
c. Luke 8: 2-3

20. Jochebed:
a. Ex. 6:20
b. Ex. 4:11
c. Ex. 21:1

21. Leah:
a. Gen. 23:24
b. Gen. 29:21-30
c. Gen. 30:1

22. Lois:
a. II Tim. 3:2
b. II Tim. 5:11
c. II Tim. 1:5

23. Lydia:
a. Acts 3:2
b. Acts 16:14-15
c. Acts 1:1

24. Mary Magdalene:
a.   Mark 16:9
b.   Mark 12:11
c.   Mark 11:10

25. Martha:
a.   John 3:14
b.   John 2:11
c.   John 11:1

26. Mary, Mother of Jesus:
a.   Acts 10:10
b.   Acts 2:30
c.   Acts 3:11

27. Micah:
a.   Gen. 11:27-29
b.   Gen. 2:11
c.   Acts 2:2

28. Miriam:
a.   Numbers 1:5
b.   Numbers 26:59
c.   Numbers 10:11

29. Peninnah:
a.   I Sam. 10:11
b.   I Sam. 5:11
c.   I Sam. 1:2-7

30. Phebe:
a. Rom. 16:1
b. Rom. 5:11
c. Rom. 6:11

31. Priscilla:
a. Rom. 1:16
b. Rom. 5:11
c. Rom. 16:3

32. Rachel:
a. Gen. 15:11
b. Gen. 29:6,16,18
c. Gen. 11:15

33. Rahab:
a. Joshua 2:1
b. Joshua 3:2
c. Joshua 3:10

34. Rebekah:
a. Gen. 24:15-16
b. Gen. 16:11
c. Ex. 21:1

35. Ruth:
a. Book of Esther
b. Book of Ruth
c. Ex. 4:11

36. Salome:
a. Mark 15:11
b. Mark 16:1
c. Mark 11:15

37. Sapphira:
a. Acts 4:11
b. Acts 10:11
c. Acts 5:1-10

38. Sarah:
a. Gen. 10:11
b. Gen. 11:10
c. Gen. 11:29

39. Tabitha:
a. Acts 9:36-43
b. Acts 8,11
c. Acts 10:11

40. Tamar
a. Gen. 10:11
b. II Sam. 13:1-33
c. II Sam. 12:11

41. Vashti:
a. Esther 1:1
b. Esther 1:11
c. Ruth 1:11

42. Zipporah:
a. Gen. 30:28
b. Exodus 2:2
c. Exodus 20:10

OLD
TESTAMENT

Where are these well known passages found?
(Choose a, b or c for correct answer)

1. The sacrifice passage concerning Isaac.
a. Genesis 32:1
b. Genesis 22
c. Genesis 10:2

2. Crossing the Red Sea
a. Exodus 11
b. Exodus 13
c. Exodus 14

3. The Ten Commandments.
a. Exodus 20
b. Exodus 13
c. Exodus 14

4. Concerning Gideon and his army.
a. Judges 9
b. Judges 7-8
c. Judges 10

5. Sampson and Delilah.
a. Judges 5
b. Exodus 1:2
c. Judges 10

6. David and Goliath.
a. I Sam. 17
b. I Sam. 19
c. I Sam. 22

7. The wisdom of Solomon,
a. I Kings 16
b. I Kings 5
c. I Kings 3

8. Jeremiah at the potter's house.
a. Jer. 10
b. Jer 18
c. Jer 22

9. Ezekiel in the valley of the dry bones.
a. Ezekiel 22
b. Ezekiel 37
c. Ezekiel 30

10. Daniel in the Lion's den.
a. Dan. 6
b. Dan. 10
c. Dan 11

11. Jonah in the belly of the big fish.
a. Jonah 5
b. Jonah 10
c. Jonah 2

12. A time to be born and a time to die.
a.   Eccl. 1:12
b.   Eccl. 3:1-8
c.   Eccl. 4:2-9

13. Though God slay me, yet will I hope in him.
a.   Job 10:11
b.   Job 13:15
c.   Job 10:11

14. The fear of the Lord is the beginning of knowlege.
a.   Prov. 3:2
b.   Prov. 4:5
c.   Prov. 1:7

15. Fear God and keep his commandments.
a.   Eccl. 10:11
b.   Eccl. 12:13
c.   Eccl. 12:20

16. Comfort ye, comfort ye, my people, says your God.
a.   Isaiah 40:5
b.   Isaiah 40:1
c.   Isaiah 45:11

17. I will put my law in their minds and write it on their hearts.
a.   Jer. 10:11
b.   Jer. 15:13
c.   Jer. 31:33

18. The Lord's compassions never fail.
a. Lam. 3:22
b. Lam. 4:5
c. Exodus 3:1

19. Salvation comes from the Lord.
a. Jonah 10:2
b. Daniel 5:2
c. Jonah 2:9

20. The righteous will live by his faith.
a. Habakkuk 2:4
b. Daniel 10:11
c. Genesis 10:1

21. Return to me, and I will return to you.
a. Malachi 2:10
b. Malachi 3:7
c. Job 3:11

22. Habakkuk said; O Lord how long shall I cry and thou wilt not hear?
a. Daniel 10:11
b. Hab. 1:2
c. Hab 2:11

23. Hezekiah prayed and wept and the Lord heard and added 15 years to his life.
a. II Kings 10:11
b. II Kings 20:5
c. II Kings 11:10

24. Woe unto them that are at ease in Zion.
a. I Kings 10:2
b. Amos 6:1
c. Ezekiel 33:28

25. God made a covenant with Noah not to destroy the earth again by water.
a. Genesis 2:13
b. Genesis 10:11
c. Genesis 9:13

26. The three sons of Noah.
a. Genesis 37:1
b. Genesis 9:18
c. Genesis 30:6

27. Thou shalt have none other gods before me.
a. Deut. 4:5
b. Deut. 5:7
c. Deut. 10:11

28. The angel of the Lord appears to Moses in a flaming bush.
a. Exodus 10:1
b. Exodus 3:2
c. Genesis 3:2

29. Joshua prayed for the sun and moon to stand still and the Lord made it happen.
a. Joshua 3:11
b. Joshua 10:13
c. Joshua 11:10

30. Thus saith the Lord: I AM THE FIRST AND I AM THE LAST AND BESIDE ME THERE IS NO GOD.

a.   Genesis 10:11
b.   Isaiah 44:6
c.   Isaiah 40:2

Where are these
WORDS SPOKEN
BY JESUS found?

(Choose a, b or c for correct answer)

1. *Nevertheless not as I will, but as thou wilt.*
a. Matt. 2:11
b. Matt. 26:39
c. Mark 2:13

2. *Before the cock crow, thou shalt deny me thrice.*
a. John 3:10
b. Luke 3:2
c. Luke 22:61

3. *Heaven and earth shall pass away; but my words shall not pass away.*
a. Luke 1:11
b. Luke 21:33
c. Matt. 10:11

4. *It is written, My house is the house of prayer: but ye have made it a den of thieves.*
a. Luke 20:2
b. Matt. 20:10
c. Luke 10:46

5. *Behold, your house is left unto you desolate; Blessed is he that cometh in the name of the Lord.*
a. Luke 13:35
b. Luke 30:1
c. Luke 14:11

6. *Martha, Martha, thou art careful and troubled about many things: But one thing is needful: and Mary hath chosen that part which shall not be taken away from her.*
a. Mark 3:2
b. Luke 10:11
c. Matt. 3:2

7. *Every kingdom divided against itself is brought to desolation; and a house divided against a house falleth.*
a. Luke 11:17
b. Matt. 11:2
c. John 3:12

8. *Foxes have holes, and birds of the air have nests; but the Son of man hath not where to lay his head.*
a. John 3:12
b. Matt. 2:5
c. Luke 9:58

9. *Among those that are born of woman there is not a greater prophet than John the Baptist: but he that is least in the Kingdom of God is greater than he.*
   a. Luke 4:12
   b. Luke 7:28
   c. Luke 10:1

10. *Judge not, and ye shall not be judged: condemn not and ye shall not be condemned: forgive and ye shall be forgiven.*
   a. Luke 13:2
   b. Matt. 10:11
   c. Luke 6:37

11. *I come not to call the righteous, but sinners to repentance.*
   a. John 10:11
   b. Luke 5:32
   c. Luke 14:2

12. *Verily I say unto you, No prophet is accepted in his own country.*
   a. Luke 4:24
   b. Luke 13:13
   c. Luke 10:11

13. *It is written, That man shall not live by bread alone, but every word of God.*
   a. Matt. 4:4
   b. Luke 4:4
   c. John 4:4

14. *Go into all the world, and preach the gospel to every creature.*
a. John 3:15
b. Mark 16:15
c. Luke 5:4

15. *Suffer the little children to come unto me, and forbid them not: for of such is the Kingdom of God.*
a. Mark 10:1
b. Mark 10:4
c. Matt. 5:10

16. *For what shall it profit a man, if he shall gain the whole world, and lose his own soul?*
a. Matt. 3:5
b. Mark 9:10
c. Mark 8:36

17. *Marvel not that I said unto thee, Ye must be born again.*
a. John 4:1
b. John 3:7
c. John 10:10

18. *God is a Spirit and they that worship him must worship Him in Spirit and in truth.*
a. Matt. 11:12
b. Jihn 1:11
c. John4:24

19. *Search the scriptures; for in them ye think ye have eternal life: and they are they which testify of me.*
a. Luke 4:11
b. John 1:11
c. John 5:39

20. *All that the Father giveth me shall come to me; and him that cometh to me I will in no wise cast out.*
a. John 6:37
b. John 4:10
c. Matt. 1:11

21. *He that is without sin among you, let him first cast a stone at her.*
a. Matt. 1:10
b. Luke 1:11
c. John 8:7

22. *If ye continue in my word, then ye are my disciples indeed; and ye know the truth, and the truth shall make you free.*
a. John 3:14
b. John 8:31
c. John 9:1

23. *I am the good Shepherd: the good Shepherd giveth his life for his sheep.*
a. Matt. 24:1
b. Luke 1:14
c. John 10:11

24. *I am the resurrection and the life: he that believeth in me, though he were dead, yet shall he live.*
a. John 11:25
b. John 10:11
c. Matt. 13:1

25. *Come unto me, all ye that labor and are heavy laden, and I will give you rest.*
a. Matt. 3:14
b. Matt. 11:28
c. Mark 3:3

26. *Take therefore no thought for the morrow: for the morrow shall take thoughts for the things of itself. Sufficient unto the day is the evil thereof.*
a. Matt. 3:11
b. Matt. 24:1
c. Matt. 6:34

27. *Let your light so shine before men, that they may see your good works, and glorify your Father which is in heaven.*
a. Matt. 5:1
b. Mark 3:10
c. Matt. 5:16

28. *Get thee hence, Satan: for it is written, Thou shalt worship the Lord thy God, and him only shalt thou serve.*
a. Matt. 4:10
b. Matt. 3:10
c. Matt. 4:17

29. *Take heed and beware of the leaven of the Pharisees and the Sadducees.*
a. Mark 3:10
b. Matt. 16:6
c. Matt. 3:11.

30. *If I then, your Lord and Master have washed your feet; ye also ought to wash one another's feet.*
a. John 3:16
b. John 13:14
c. John 5:1

NEW
TESTAMENT

WHERE ARE THESE PASSAGES FOUND?
(Choose from a, b and c for correct answers)

1. The birth of Jesus Christ.
a. Matt. 2
b. Matt. 1:15
c. Matt. 5

2. Christ's first miracle at the wedding in Cana.
a. Matt. 8:13
b. John 2
c. John 5

3. Christ is baptized by John the Baptist.
a. Matt. 2:10
b. Matt. 3:15
c. Matt. 2:11

4. The appointment of Christ's Apostles.
a. Matt. 1:11
b. Mark 1:10
c. Matt. 10:1-4

5. Sermon on the Mount.
a. Matt. 5-7
b. Matt. 6-8
c. Matt. 3-10

6. The parable of the sower.
a. Matt. 13:3-9
b. Luke 5
c. Luke 8

7. Feeding the multitude.
a. Mark 6
b. Mark 8
c. Luke 2

8. The Lord's Last Supper.
a. Luke 22
b. Mark 14
c. Matt. 26:26

9. Christ's betrayal by Judas.
a. Mark 14:1
b. Mark 14:10
c. Mark 20:11

10. Christ's crucifixion.
a. Mark 15:24
b. Matt. 27:35
c. Luke 3

11. Christ's resurrection.
a. Mark 15
b. Matt. 28
c. Matt. 30

12. Conversion of Paul.
a.   I Cor. 9:16-17
b.   Luke 3
c.   Ephesians 3:7-9

13. Day of Pentecost.
a.   Acts 10
b.   Acts 1
c.   Acts 2

14. Christ gave the apostles power and auth-ority over all devils, and to cure diseases.
a.   Luke 9:1
b.   Luke 1:15
c.   Luke 10

15. Shortest verse: Jesus wept.
a.   John 2:19
b.   John 11:35
c.   Luke 20:1

16. The qualifications of a bishop.
a.   Matt. 2:16
b.   I Tim. 3:2-7
c.   I Tim. 3:3

17. The qualifications of a deacon.
a.   I Tim. 8:10
b.   I Tim. 3:8-13
c.   I Tim. 9:1

18. Pure religion and undefiled before God.
a. James 2:10
b. James 1:27
c. James 3:10

19. The love of money is the root of all evil.
a. Luke 2:3
b. I Tim. 6:10
c. Mark 5:11

20. Christian duties.
a. Titus 1:16
b. Philemon 1:10
c. Titus 2 & 3

21. The seven churches of Asia.
a. Jude
b. Revelation
c. Philemon

22. The Great White Throne Judgement
a. Rev. 1:15
b. Rev. 6
c. Rev. 20:11-15

❖ **AMEN** ❖

BIBLE QUIZ

Part II

Answers

ANGELS
(answers)

1. B	6. C	11. B	16. A
2. C	7. A	12. C	17. B
3. B	8. C	13. A	18. B
4. A	9. B	14. C	19. A
5. B	10. A	15. B	20. B

NEW TESTAMENT PASSAGES
(answers)

1. A	7. B	13. C	19. B
2. B	8. C	14. A	20. C
3. B	9. B	15. B	21. B
4. C	10. A&B	16. B	22. C
5. A	11. B	17. B	
6. A	12. A&C	18. B	

PSALMS
(answers)

1. A	8. C	15. B	22. C
2. C	9. B	16. C	23. B
3. C	10. A	17. B	24. A
4. B	11. B	18. C	25. B
5. B	12. C	19. A	
6. A	13. B	20. C	
7. B	14. A	21. B	

WOMEN OF THE BIBLE

(Answers)

1. C	22. C
2. B	23. B
3. C	24. A
4. A	25. C
5. B	26. B
6. B	27. A
7. A	28. B
8. B	29. C
9. C	30. A
10. A	31. C
11. C	32. B
12. B	33. A
13. C	34. A
14. A	35. B
15. B	36. B
16. B	37. C
17. A	38. C
18. B	39. A
19. C	40. B
20. A	41. B
21. B	42. B

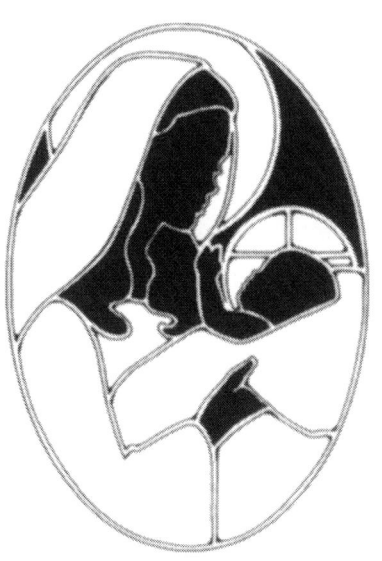

V. L. Reece

PHRASES
(answers)

*(Some Old Testament
Phrases used today)*

1. A	5. A
2. A	6. C
3. C	7. A
4. B	

SAYINGS
(answers)

*(Some New Testament
Sayings used today)*

1. B	5. A
2. C	6. C
3. B	7. A
4. C	8. B

OLD TESTAMENT
(answers)

1. B	9. B	17. C	25. C
2. C	10. A	18. A	26. B
3. A	11. C	19. C	27. B
4. B	12. B	20. A	28. B
5. C	13. B	21. B	29. B
6. A	14. C	22. B	30. B
7. C	15. B	23. B	
8. B	16. B	24. B	

SPOKEN BY JESUS
(answers)

1. B	9. B	17. B	25. B
2. C	10. C	18. C	26. C
3. B	11. B	19. C	27. C
4. C	12. A	20. A	28. A
5. A	13. B	21. C	29. B
6. B	14. B	22. B	30. B
7. A	15. B	23. C	
8. C	16. C	24. A	

NOTES

NOTES

NOTES

About The Author

V. Reece is the granddaughter of a Primitive Baptist preacher with fond memories of her dad and grandpa talking "Bible" every time they were together. This kind of environment was obviously instrumental in the development of the kind of faith required to put together a work such as this collection of bible quizzes.

As a young teenager, she won a talent contest which earned her a spot on a local Country Music show where she performed and recorded her songs for several years until the development of her family became more important, and with the birth of her son, Terry Neal and then her first daughter Lee Ann, she gave up the musical career.

The next professional endeavor for V. Reece was in the field of cosmetology. At one point she owned 5 salons and a beauty college. It was at this point she was blessed with the birth of her second daughter Wynette. The involvement in the cosmetology business became a problem with the development of arthritis, and the loss of her partner in the business, her husband, Boyd Reece.

Looking for still another challenge and a way to be productive and helpful with her life, V. Reece then trained for a new career and became an asset to those she worked with in the field of respiratory therapy. Since retiring from 20 years of service in that industry Mrs. Reece is doing what she has always wanted to do...raising beautiful flowers to share bouquets with her church and friends.

So, at this point in her life, she has truly felt the urge to do something REALLY beneficial for her family and church friends. Always an avid reader and huge fan of puzzles, this author actually began this process by writing quizzes for herself! There was a special excitement and intrigue in knowing that by creating the pursuit of these answers for others brings an awesome feeling of real and worthwhile accomplishment... helping others to learn from and become more involved in the Word of God. Bravo!!

Printed in Great Britain
by Amazon